American Civics

Elections in the United States

by David Heath

Consultant:
Steven S. Smith,
Distinguished McKnight University
Professor of Political Science,
University of Minnesota

CAPSTONE BOOKS
an imprint of Capstone Press
Mankato, Minnesota

Capstone Books are published by Capstone Press
151 Good Counsel Drive, P.O. Box 669, Mankato, Minnesota 56002
http://www.capstone-press.com

Library of Congress Cataloging-in-Publication Data
Heath, David, 1948–
    Elections in the United States/by David Heath.
    p. cm.—(American civics)
    Includes bibliographical references and index.
    Contents: Discusses national, state and local elections, as well as political
parties and the electoral college.
    ISBN 0-7368-8857-8
    1. Elections—United States—Juvenile literature. 2. Political parties—United
States—Juvenile literature. 3. Civics—Juvenile literature. I. Title. II. Series.
JK1978.H4 1999
324.6'0973—DC21   98-17206
                                                                  CIP
                                                                  AC

Editorial Credits
Colleen Sexton, editor; Timothy Halldin, cover designer; Sheri Gosewisch,
    photo researcher

Photo Credits
Carol Simowitz, 20, 29
Corbis-Bettmann, 10, 13, 17
Elliot Smith, cover
Jim West/Impact Visuals, 36
Reuters/Archive Photos/Mike Segar, 6
Shaffer Photography/James L. Shaffer, 46
Unicorn Stock Photos/D&I MacDonald, 5; Rich Baker, 9; Jeff Greenberg, 18;
    ChromoSohm/Joseph Sohm, 26, 32; Jean Higgins, 40; Jim Shippee, 43
UPI/Corbis-Bettmann, 14, 22, 25, 31
Visuals Unlimited/Arthur Gurkmankin, 34; Hank Andrews, 39

2 3 4 5 6 04 03 02 01 00

Table of Contents

Fast Facts about Elections in the United States

Form of Government in the United States: Democracy

Election Day: The first Tuesday after the first Monday in November

Minimum Voting Age: 18

Year All Men Gained the Right to Vote: 1870

Year All Women Gained the Right to Vote: 1920

First U.S. Political Parties: Federalist Party and Democratic-Republican Party

Major U.S. Political Parties Today: Democratic Party and Republican Party

Election Day is the first Tuesday after the first Monday in November.

Chapter 1

Elections in a Democracy

The United States is a democracy. A democracy is a form of government in which citizens elect their leaders. Citizens elect leaders at many levels of government. They choose national leaders such as the president of the United States. They elect governors and other state leaders. Citizens also choose leaders in their cities and neighborhoods.

A Representative Government

In a democracy, every citizen can have a voice in the decisions a government makes. But it would take a long time for every citizen to vote on every issue. So citizens elect people to represent them in the government. Representatives speak

New York City Mayor Rudolph Guiliani takes the oath of office. U.S. citizens elect mayors in local elections.

and act for others. Representatives make rules and laws that affect all citizens.

People who run for elected offices are candidates. Each candidate usually has a platform. A platform states the beliefs of a person or group. Voters choose candidates whose beliefs are similar to their own. Elected officials make decisions based on their platforms. In this way, elections allow citizens to have a voice in government decisions.

Referendums

Citizens sometimes vote directly on issues that affect them. Elected officials may decide to hold referendums in which people vote on issues themselves. Referendums allow citizens to be directly involved in decisions.

Referendums usually are about important local issues. The issue might address whether to raise city taxes. The money from taxes might go to local schools or neighborhood building projects.

States also hold referendums. Citizens might vote on raising state taxes. Or they

Citizens protest an increase in taxes. Cities and states sometimes hold referendums on tax increases.

might vote on a change to a state's constitution. States base the way their governments operate on their constitution.

The Right to Vote

U.S. citizens who are at least 18 years old have the right to vote. But it was not always this way

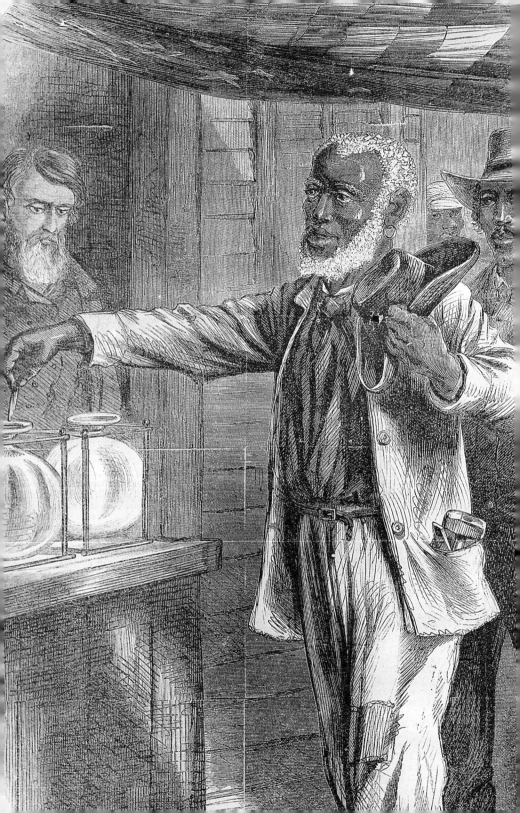

in the United States. In 1776, the only people who could vote were white men over age 21 who owned land. New laws in the mid-1800s gave all white men over age 21 the right to vote.

Congress passed the 15th Amendment to the Constitution in 1870. This amendment gave all men the right to vote. These men included African Americans. Many African Americans were slaves until 1865.

Some people still believed that former slaves and poor men did not deserve the right to vote. Many former slaves and poor men could not read or write. And most of them had little money. So some states required all men to pass reading and writing tests before they could vote. In other states, voters had to pay a tax to vote. These requirements kept many former slaves and poor men from voting.

New laws in the 1960s outlawed voting taxes and reading and writing tests. The 24th Amendment said states could not stop qualified citizens from voting. This amendment ended

African American men won the right to vote in 1870.

voting taxes. But some states still required people to take tests to qualify to vote. The Voting Rights Act stopped states from using reading and writing tests to qualify voters.

Women could not vote for many years. Women held meetings to talk about voting rights for women. Some women wrote newspaper articles about the subject. Women in many cities marched in the streets to show their beliefs. They tried to convince people that women should have the right to vote. In 1920, the 19th Amendment gave all women over age 21 the right to vote.

Congress adopted the 26th Amendment in 1971. This amendment set the voting age at 18 for national elections.

Women over age 21 won the right to vote in 1920.

Chapter 2

Political Parties

Some voters belong to political parties.
People in these groups share similar opinions
about government and important issues.
Members of a political party discuss issues
and choose their stance on the issues. Political
parties usually have platforms that state
these opinions.

Political parties work to elect candidates at
all levels of government. A political party has
more power when it has many members in
office. Once elected, party members work to
pass laws that favor their views on the issues.

Political parties help their candidates run
for election. Parties raise campaign money for
candidates. Some party members volunteer to
work for campaigns. Party members who

Political parties work to elect candidates at all levels of government.

already hold government offices show their support for candidates.

History of Political Parties

The U.S. Constitution did not include a plan for political parties in the U.S. government. But people began to form political parties in the United States during the late 1700s.

The Federalist Party was one of the first political parties in the United States. Federalists believed the United States needed a strong central government. They thought the national government should be more important than state governments.

The Democratic-Republican Party opposed the Federalists' beliefs. Democratic-Republicans believed the national government should have little power. They thought most of the power should belong to state governments.

Both the Federalist and Democratic-Republican parties broke up in the 1800s. The Democratic-Republican Party became the Democratic Party in 1840. The Federalist Party was replaced by the National Republican Party and then by the Whig

Some political parties broke up and formed new parties in the 1800s.

Party. In 1854, some Whigs and some Democrats left their parties to create the Republican Party. Today, the Democratic Party and the Republican Party are the two major political parties.

Many minor political parties exist in the United States. Some parties want to change the type of government the United States has. They do not believe the country should be a democracy. Other parties think the country should be even more democratic than it is.

New parties also have formed around certain issues such as the environment or taxes. These parties support laws that further their interests. Voters elect very few candidates from minor parties. Democrats and Republicans hold almost every national political office.

Democrats and Republicans

Many people in the United States agree with the beliefs of either the Democratic Party or the Republican Party. The beliefs of these two

Many political parties exist in the United States. Ross Perot was the Reform Party's candidate for president in 1992 and 1996.

major parties have affected many laws and government actions.

People consider the Democratic Party to be liberal. Liberals believe the government should change laws and political systems to solve problems. Many Democrats want a large national government. The Democratic Party believes the national government should set standards for the country. The party also believes the government should be responsible for the well-being of all citizens.

People consider the Republican Party to be conservative. Conservatives believe change should be gradual. They believe that making new laws is not always the best way to solve problems. The Republican Party favors a small national government. The party believes state and local governments should set standards for citizens. Many Republicans believe the government should help citizens do only those things they cannot do on their own.

The donkey is a symbol of the Democratic Party. The Democratic Party is one of the largest U.S. parties.

Chapter 3

National Elections

Voters choose the president, vice president, and members of Congress in national elections. The Senate and the House of Representatives make up Congress. National elections take place every two years.

Different positions come up for election at different times. Voters elect a president and a vice president every four years. Voters elect representatives to the House of Representatives every two years. Citizens do not elect all senators at the same time. Senators serve for six years. Voters elect one-third of the Senate every two years.

Primary Elections

Primaries are elections in which registered party members choose their candidates for

Voters elect a president and vice president every four years.

23

office. Each political party may have many people who want to run for the same office. Members elect one candidate from their party to run for each office. In the final election, winners of the primary election for each party run against each other.

Voters directly choose candidates in most primaries. But presidential primaries are different. Citizens' votes actually elect party delegates in presidential primaries. These representatives promise to vote for a certain candidate at the party's national convention. Delegates choose presidential candidates at these meetings.

Caucuses

Caucuses are another way to choose candidates. Some states hold these meetings instead of primaries. Each party holds many caucuses across a state to discuss issues for party platforms. Voters can voice their opinions and bring up issues that interest them.

Voters gather at a Democratic Party caucus in Iowa in 1988.

Voters also elect delegates at caucuses. Each caucus can elect a certain number of delegates. People at the meeting divide into groups that support each candidate. The candidate who has the most supporters wins the most delegates. Voters then elect people from each group to serve as delegates. These delegates attend state and national party conventions.

Party Conventions

Political parties hold national conventions for two purposes. Parties adopt their platforms. Parties also endorse their candidates for president and vice president. These two candidates campaign together as running mates.

The Democratic Party and the Republican Party hold the largest conventions. The parties hold conventions every four years before presidential elections. The conventions last about five days. Voters across the country can see many convention events on TV.

Political parties hold national conventions. The Republican Party held their convention in San Diego in 1996.

Delegates, party officials, candidates, and news reporters gather in large convention centers. They listen to speeches from the candidates. Other party members also speak. The delegates nominate candidates to run in the general election. The person with the most nominations becomes the party's endorsed candidate. Candidates accept their nominations in speeches.

General Elections

General elections for national offices take place in November. The elections are always held on the first Tuesday following the first Monday of the month.

Citizens throughout the country cast their votes for president and vice president. People also vote for senators and representatives for their own states. Voters can choose among candidates from any political party. Citizens do not have to vote for candidates from a certain party.

Officials count all the votes after voting places close on election day. The candidates who receive the most votes win the popular vote.

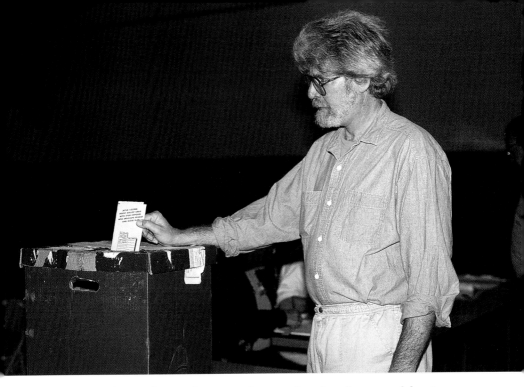

Citizens throughout the country cast votes for president and vice president.

Electoral College

U.S. citizens do not directly elect the president and vice president on election day. Instead, citizens vote for electors. Each of these representatives has promised to vote for a certain candidate. Electors are members of the Electoral College. The U.S. Constitution established the Electoral College.

Each state has different ways of selecting electors. States choose as many electors as they have members of Congress. That number depends on the state's population. States with more people have more members of Congress and more electors.

Electors gather in their states in the December after the election. They use the popular vote to decide how many electoral votes each candidate will receive. The candidate with the greatest number of popular votes receives all the electoral votes from that state.

Officials send the electoral votes from their states to Washington, D.C., to be counted by Congress. A candidate must receive at least 270 of the 538 electoral votes to win the presidential election. It is possible that no candidate will receive a majority of votes. If this happens, the House of Representatives chooses a president from among the top three candidates. The Senate chooses the vice president.

Many people believe the United States does not need the Electoral College. They believe that the candidates who win the popular vote should always become president and vice president.

Officials from each state send electoral votes to Congress.

Chapter 4

State and Local Elections

Representatives elected to state and local governments work close to home. They make laws and rules that directly affect their communities. Their work affects the daily lives of citizens as much as the work of national representatives.

State Elections

Most state governments have branches like those of the national government. The governor heads the state government. The state legislature makes state laws. The state courts decide whether these laws agree with state constitutions. Citizens choose people to hold these government offices during state elections.

Citizens choose their state government in state elections.

Pennsylvanians attend a Democratic Party rally. Candidates for state offices usually belong to a political party.

Candidates for state offices belong to political parties. They run for election on platforms that support the beliefs of their parties. Citizens vote in primary elections to choose candidates from each party. These candidates run in the general elections.

States set guidelines for the terms of government officials. Most states elect a governor every four years. Vermont and New Hampshire choose a new governor every two years. Members of state legislatures usually are elected every two years or every four years. Voters elect judges in some states. The terms of judges vary greatly. Judges are appointed for life in some states.

Citizens also vote about state issues in referendums. Most state referendums are about taxes. People may vote for or against raising taxes. The money from higher taxes may pay for social services, education, new highways, or new prisons.

Local Elections

Citizens elect city and county officials in local elections. Voters may elect mayors, city council members, county sheriffs, or school board members. These officials make decisions about county, city, and neighborhood issues.

Some local candidates belong to political parties. These candidates run on platforms that support the beliefs of their parties. But many local candidates are independent. They run for office based on their own beliefs. Voters may know local candidates personally.

The local election process varies from city to city and from county to county. Voters usually elect local officials on election day. Citizens also vote in local referendums on issues such as road improvements and school funding.

POLLING PLACE

VOTE HERE

JAMES H. BRADLEY
CITY CLERK

Polls Close 8:00 p.m.

Chapter 5

Election Day

Citizens vote at polling places on election day. Voters usually go to polling places in their neighborhoods. Polling places may be in schools, churches, or government buildings. Election boards in each state make rules for how polling places operate on election day.

Preparing for Election Day

Many people work to prepare polling places for election day. Some people print ballots. People mark their votes on ballots. Other workers set up machines that count votes. Workers also set up tables and organize the voting process.

Some workers prepare lists of registered voters for each polling place. Registered voters are people signed up to vote before election

Citizens vote at polling places on election day.

day. The registered voter lists help workers at polling places make sure the voting process is fair. Workers make sure each citizen votes only once.

Voting

Most polling places open early in the morning and stay open into the evening. This makes voting convenient for most citizens. Many people vote before or after work.

Voters first check in. Workers make sure voters are legally registered. People can register before elections. In some states, people can register at polling places on election day. Voters sign their names in registers to show that they have voted.

Some polling places use paper ballots. Workers hand out ballots and give voters directions for marking them. Voters then go into private booths to mark their ballots. The booths usually have curtains or tall walls. The booths prevent people from seeing which candidates other voters select.

Some polling places use polling machines.

People vote by marking an X or by filling in a box next to the chosen candidate's name. Voters may put their marked ballots into locked ballot boxes. Workers sometimes send the ballots through a machine to count the votes.

Other polling places use voting machines instead of paper ballots. Most voting machines are in large booths. Inside the booths, voters

select candidates by flipping switches next to their names. Voters then pull a large handle near the switches to record their entire ballot. Polling places in large cities often use voting machines. These polling places have many votes to count. The machine keeps track of the number of votes each candidate receives.

Voters who are out of town on election day may fill out absentee ballots. They must send in their ballots before election day.

Counting the Votes

After the polls close in the evening, workers keep ballot boxes locked. They take the ballot boxes to a central polling location. Election officials count the votes for each candidate. The officials add absentee ballots and the votes counted by voting machines to the totals. Officials often use computers to keep track of all the votes.

Officials send the final totals to election offices for city, county, state, or national governments. Election officials add all the totals together and announce the winners.

Workers at polling places keep votes in locked ballot boxes.

Words to Know

ballot (BAL-uht)—a piece of paper on which a person marks a vote

candidate (CAN-dih-dayt)—a person who runs for elected office

caucus (KAW-kuhs)—a gathering of people who elect delegates and discuss issues for party platforms

delegate (DEHL-uh-geht)—a person who represents other people at a convention

electoral college (ee-lehk-TOHR-uhl KAHL-uhj)—the group of people that elects the president and vice president after the general election

platform (PLAT-fohrm)—a statement of beliefs

primary election (PRY-mar-ee ee-LEHK-shuhn)—an election in which voters choose the party candidates who will run for office

referendum (rehf-er-EHN-duhm)—a public vote on an important issue

Citizens often register to vote before election day.

To Learn More

Brill, Marlene Targ. *Let Women Vote!* Spotlight on American History. Brookfield, Conn.: Millbrook Press, 1996.

Feinberg, Barbara Silberdick. *Electing the President.* Inside Government. New York: Twenty-First Century Books, 1995.

Henry, Christopher. *The Electoral College.* A First Book. New York: Franklin Watts, 1996.

Henry, Christopher. *Presidential Conventions.* A First Book. New York: Franklin Watts, 1996.

Maestro, Betsy C. *The Voice of the People.* New York: Lothrop, Lee & Shepard Books, 1996.

Steins, Richard. *Our Elections.* I Know America. Brookfield, Conn.: Millbrook Press, 1994.

Useful Addresses

Democratic National Committee
430 South Capitol Street SE
Washington, DC 20003-4024

Federal Election Commission
999 E Street NW
Washington, DC 20463-0002

League of Women Voters
1730 M Street NW
Washington, DC 20036-4508

Republican National Committee
310 First Street SE
Washington, DC 20003-1801

Internet Sites

The Democratic National Committee
http://www.democrats.org

Elections in American Memory
http://lcweb2.loc.gov/ammem/ndlpedu/features/
   election/election.html

Electoral College
http://www.nara.gov/fedreg/electcoll/index.
   html#top

Kids Voting USA
http://www.kidsvotingusa.org

League of Women Voters
http://www.lwv.org

The Republican National Committee
http://www.rnc.org

Candidates campaign before elections.

Index